Aunia Kahn
Russell J. Moon

LOWBROW TAROT

An Artistic Collaborative Effort in Honor of Tarot

Schiffer Publishing Ltd

4880 Lower Valley Road • Atglen, PA 19310

Other Schiffer Books By The Author:
Silver Era Tarot   978-0-7643-3438-2 $24.99

Designed by Justin Watkinson
Type set in Bernhard Tango Swash/NewBskvll BT

ISBN: 978-0-7643-4233-2
Printed in China

Schiffer Books are available at special discounts for bulk purchases for sales promotions or premiums. Special editions, including personalized covers, corporate imprints, and excerpts can be created in large quantities for special needs. For more information contact the publisher:

Published by Schiffer Publishing, Ltd.
4880 Lower Valley Road
Atglen, PA 19310
Phone: (610) 593-1777; Fax: (610) 593-2002
E-mail: Info@schifferbooks.com

For the largest selection of fine reference books on this and related subjects, please visit our website at **www.schifferbooks.com**
We are always looking for people to write books on new and related subjects. If you have an idea for a book, please contact us at proposals@schifferbooks.com

This book may be purchased from the publisher. Please try your bookstore first.
You may write for a free catalog.

In Europe, Schiffer books are distributed by
Bushwood Books
6 Marksbury Ave.
Kew Gardens
Surrey TW9 4JF England
Phone: 44 (0) 20 8392 8585;
Fax: 44 (0) 20 8392 9876
E-mail: info@bushwoodbooks.co.uk
Website: www.bushwoodbooks.co.uk

Dedicated to
the love of divination
and self exploration.
May you find a close
connection with your soul.

CONTENTS

THE LOWBROW TAROT PROJECT

INSPIRATION

Tarot and the revelations that countless people have come to seek from their use inspired me to launch The Lowbrow Tarot Project. Since the completion of my Silver Era Tarot deck, which explored every tarot suit plus the Major Arcana, artists have complimented my ability to complete such a large individual project. Many expressed a wish to have done the same thing, but time and ongoing commitments seemed to prevent the vast majority.

When I put the wheels in motion, the concept of this new project needed a simpler incarnation: one artist to one card of the Major Arcana. There were no restrictions, except that the work would need to be a new original piece and be focused around the card they were given or wanted to complete. The original call for art hit the streets with an overwhelming response, with close to 1,000 submissions received by the final submission due date.

The arduous task of choosing only twenty-two artists cemented the realization of how unique a project this was becoming. Visitors to La Luz De Jesus Gallery would see an exhibition culminating multiple mediums in different formats and styles which encased each artist's original view of what Tarot means to them, individually. As the project came to full fruition, I could not express enough my honest appreciation and thanks to all the artists who put their talents to full-force to meet the deadlines to get this amazing event to the public. To them, and the countless others that submitted, assisted, encouraged, and challenged us, I say thank you.

~Curator and Artist Aunia Kahn

PROJECT SUCCESS

The Lowbrow Tarot Project showcased 23 amazing artists who used their creative genius and unique style to take on the 22 Major Arcana [plus the card back] and create 23 new works of art in the rugged glow of the lowbrow art movement that debuted at La Luz De Jesus Gallery, Los Angeles, California, on October 1, 2010.

Culver City, CA October 16, 2009 – *The Lowbrow Tarot Project* will showcase 23 artists who will use their creative and unique styles to take on the tarot 22 Major Arcana and original card back totaling 23 new works of art in the rugged glow of the lowbrow art movement to be displayed in an exhibition at La Luz de Jesus on October 1, 2010.

The group exhibition will feature 23 new and original works by renowned and accomplished artists Carrie Ann Baade, Christopher Ulrich, Edith Lebeau, Cate Rangel, Kris Kuksi, Chris Mars, Christopher Umana, Christopher Conn Askew, Brian M. Viveros, Claudia Drake, Heather Watts, Molly Crabapple, David Stoupakis, Laurie Lipton, Patrick "Star 27" Deignan, Chet Zar, Jessica Joslin, Danni Shinya Luo, Jennybird Alcantara, Angie Mason, Scott G. Brooks, Aunia Kahn, and Daniel Martin Diaz.

Curator and artist Aunia Kahn developed the project after the completion of her own 78-card *Silver Era Tarot* deck and believed most artists would enjoy the exploration of divination without the commitment to a larger, overwhelming project. In addition, a hardcover tabletop book and full-color Tarot card deck of the work will be available.

La Luz De Jesus is located at 4633 Hollywood Boulevard, Los Angeles, CA 90232, and will host the show starting October 1, 2010 with a free opening reception with the artists and public from 8 p.m. – 11 p.m. and will run until November 1, 2010.

Official Promotional Event Flyer by Aunia Kahn

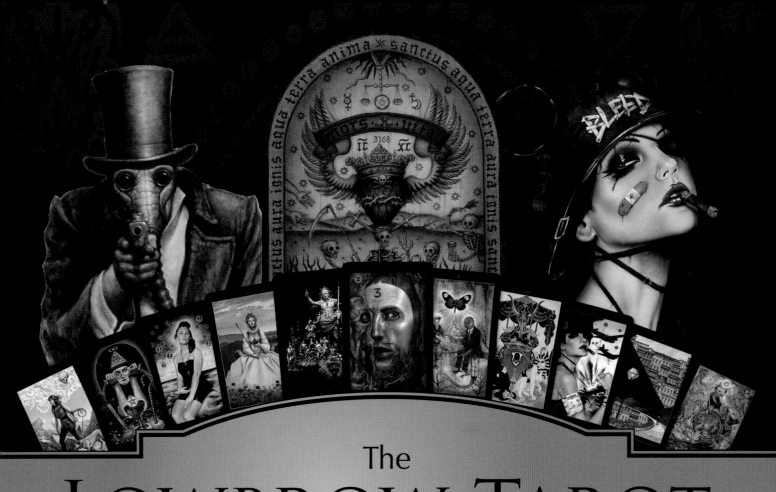

The
LOWBROW TAROT
ARTISTS' GALLERY

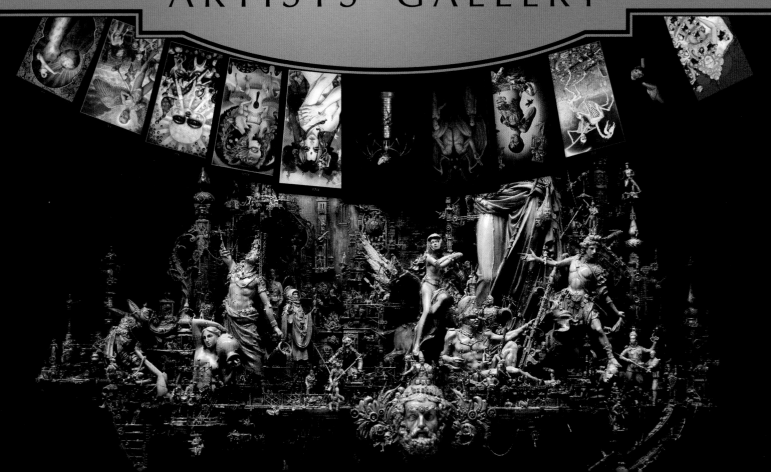

DANIEL MARTIN DIAZ

www.danielmartindiaz.com

"Apocalypse"

THE LOWBROW TAROT CARD BACK

One of my earliest memories as a child was the way death and religion played an important role in my family's life. My parents were born in Mexico with traditional beliefs, and their beliefs made their way into my subconscious. The fact that many of those beliefs seemed to render no logical explanation has also influenced me. These unanswered questions find a home in my work, which evokes the mystery, fear and irony of those vivid memories of my past. I do not claim to understand these questions. I just paint and let them reveal themselves to me.

"Veritas Lux Mea"

"Mysterium Tremendum"

"Apocalyptic Beast"

"Celestial Christ"

"Captus Animus"

"Elegy"

"Hidden Prophecies"

"Fatima Prophecies"

"Christ and the Fallen Angel"

"Christ and the Two Thieves"

"The Resonator"

"Mystery of the Apocalypse"

"Mysteries Secrets"

"The Seven Sorrows"

CARRIE ANN BAADE

www.carrieannbaade.com

"The Bride Stripping the Bachelors Bare"

"Explaining Death to a Rabbit"

·0·
THE FOOL

The Fool carries only a bag upon her back and in her hand a leash to lead her dog. The leash subtly makes the sign of the infinity symbol as our intrepid traveler takes a step that will lead her off the rational path and into the unknown. Fearless, she embarks on this experience, the sun radiates at her back; she does not fear or acknowledge the grinning skull that lights her way. It is suggestive of her "crazy wisdom" that she need not acknowledge fate.

"The Involuntary Thoughts of Lady Caroline Dubois"

"Joy and Sorrow"

"Lady or Tiger"

"Perilous Compassion of the Honey Queen"

"Queen Bitch"

"Red Queen"

"True Love on the Eve of the Apocalypse"

"Temptation of the Penitent Medusa"

"The Plague"

"A Caterpillar Explains the Little Death"

"The Magician"

Christopher Ulrich

www.christopherulrich.com

"Triumph"

"Choice"

What I found interesting was that The Magician was the first artwork I had to paint in 2010 and the last one to be exhibited that year. I was working on my Illuminator series that I showed on my birthday in August and also had my Demoneater exhibit. This had a special meaning for me personally since my work deals with alchemical concepts. I found the Magician to be the perfect card for me at that time, and exactly what I needed to meditate on as I began on my next big project. As I started to envision the first of the Major Arcana, I heard the music of Amadeus Mozart playing in my head. Then I was in a theater during 1921 watching Alexander perform and then Aleister Crowley took me behind the stage shouting "Charlatan!" Then the picture came to me, and the secrets were revealed, here I will attempt to decode it:

The serpent bites it's own tail, a perfect circle. The end and the beginning become one. This is the present moment in the journey, the center point of the crossroad. Behold the Magician, the Con Man, the androgynous infinite player who dances with light and shadow! "Do what thou wilt shall be the whole of the law." The central figure in the infamous pose of the "beast" teaches the art of choice, the will causing change. Each person has the right to fulfill their own destiny is the Magician's message. His blue skin is the color of the dead man brought back to life, the drowned magi who returns from the abyss. The background is a blazing purple; the royal color that symbolizes everything is permissible. The cube that cannot be seen unfolds into a flat cross; the Grail (cups) is placed at the yellow center (the sun). The pentacle levitates inside it as the holy host and cosmic flames engulf the foreground. The black square is closest to the viewer, the seeker, the one who is at the mercy of the trick. The green right square is the path of Osiris the dead god of vegetation; his staff (wands) is the symbol of the pharaoh or the great shepherd. The left blue square holds the dagger (swords) and is the symbol of the sky god, that which cuts away illusion. The alchemical red square is the crown color, the high achievement that faces the Magician. The salamander is the life within the fire. This is the consciousness card, the here and now, the moment one must break from the old wounds and the ego, for a new beginning to occur.

"Destiny"

"Eternity"

"Evolution"

"Expulsion"

"Fate"

"Fertility"

"Grace"

"Harmony"

"Humility"

"Infinity"

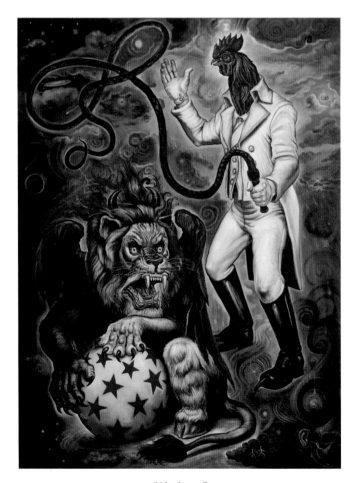

"Obedience"

"Purity"

"Resurrection"

"Revelation"

"The High Priestess"

EDITH LEBEAU

www.edithlebeau.com

·II·
THE HIGH PRIESTESS

I enjoyed doing my interpretation of The High Priestess card from the Rider-Waite Tarot deck. I kept in mind that The High Priestess card is related to our feminine side, to knowledge, mystery and unconscious awareness. She is the guardian of the unconscious. The High Priestess can also be related to Persephone, who was traveling between our world and the underworld every six months because she eats pomegranate seeds.

"The Red Bird"

"Blue Orchid"

"The Beekeeper"

"Calypso"

25

"The Guardian"

"Ode to Ladybird"

"Self Portrait"

"Cio Cio San"

"The Ocean"

"The Twins"

"The Empress"

CATE
RANGEL

www.caterangel.com

"Daydream"

The Empress, seated on her throne surrounded by the bountiful earth that she is meant to represent, is a symbol of fertility, patience, sensuality, love, and creation. She is a life force, Mother Nature, and gives birth to all creation. She is the goddess of abundance and beautiful things. While she is pregnant with opportunity, ideas, love, and creativity, there is also a need for patience and nurturing that comes with allowing things to gestate and grow. The field of ripe wheat and flowers represents nourishment and nurturing, and the pomegranate suggests fertility, love, and feminine sexuality. The water is a symbol of emotion, tranquility, and expansive power, and with this force comes the necessity to be mindful of the destructive nature it can hold. The heart is an emblem of love and the stars are representative of the twelve months or Zodiac. The Empress is the giver of life and abundance, but in anger, she can also withhold.

"Vera"

"Adele"

"Kristen"

"Lacy"

"Nadine"

"Love Hurts"

"Red Ruff"

"The Shepherdess"

"Sea No Evil"

"The Emperor"

KRIS KUKSI

www.kuksi.com

Having been a history buff for so long, I couldn't help but take the opportunity to do The Emperor in the Tarot series because of how I associate with the ancient Roman emperors. Caesar just seemed like the natural pick in how I wanted to translate my addition to the Tarot series. Yet, I felt it was of good interest to depict such an Emperor among distorted, figural forms that signify an impending decline or the social and political calamity that inevitably happened to ancient Rome. However, in this case, I did not wish to be too literal about ancient Rome, but more so, directed towards the vulnerability of highly advanced civilizations. There is a constant and consistent wave, the rise and fall of societies throughout world history. When I produced this work, it felt like an easily interpreted statement, my contribution that says it takes bold persons to keep a country or empire together. A fight for the survival of the state can be an empire's greatest battle; for decline can readily happen from within. Caesar explains this very simply: "As a rule, men worry more about what they can't see than about what they can."

KRIS KUKSI

"Church Tank Type 8"

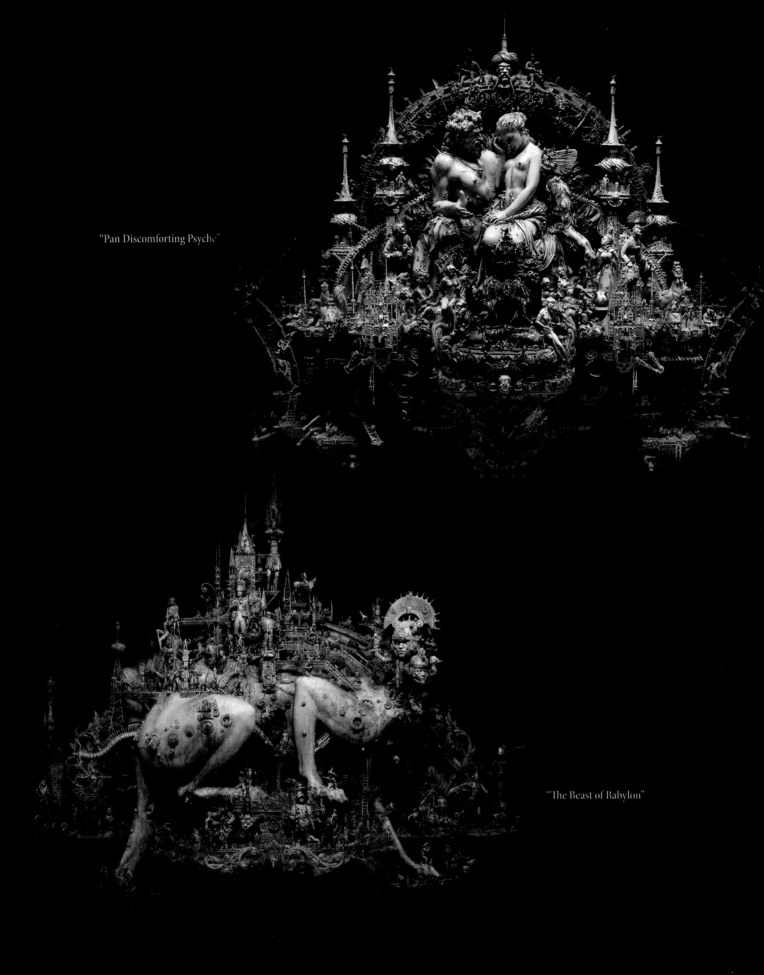

"Pan Discomforting Psyche"

"The Beast of Babylon"

"A Heroic Abduction"

"A Neo-Roman Landscape"

"Eros at Play"

"Oedipus in Contemplation"

"The Retreat of Daphne"

"A Rather Noble Cock"

"Ode to Herculaneum"

"Gemini"

"Portrait of a Neo-Roman Empress"

"The Three Disgraces"

41

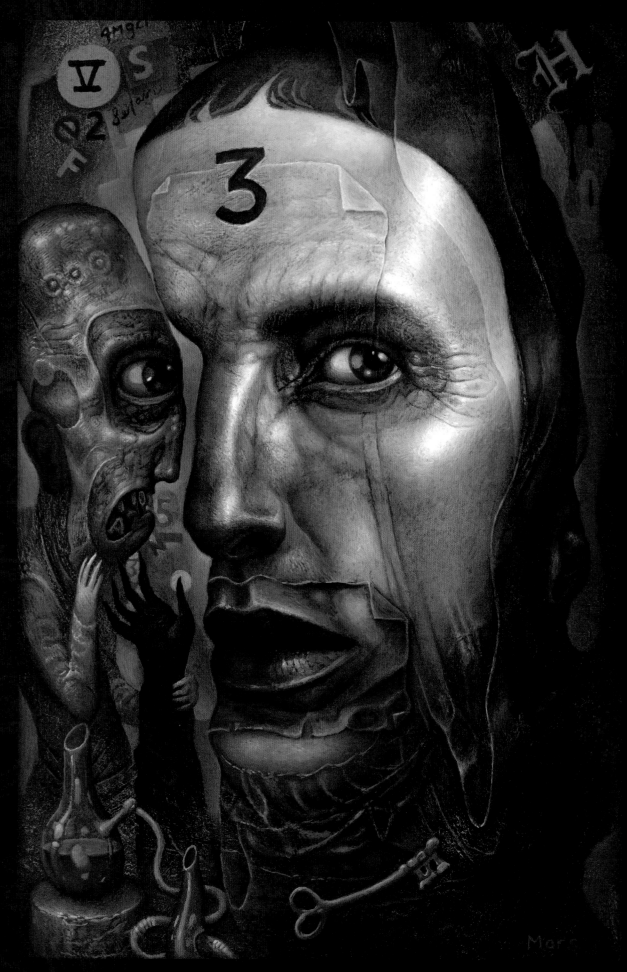

"The Hierophant"

CHRIS MARS

www.chrismarspublishing.com

"Victus Mortuus"

It is appropriate that a teacher should be a leader – presuming the teacher is not corrupt. Here is The Hierophant: Teacher, leader; in position to educate, or brainwash. The Hierophant, tasked with this: To bring the spiritual down to Earth to deal with worldly problems. A noble endeavor, yes.

But under the auspice of nobility can come manipulation. A leader may lead, or mislead. Therein lies the dichotomy of the Hierophant: To teach, but what? To steer, but heading where? The Hierophant, once denoting Taurus, The Earthly Bull, then called The Teacher. But as the church infused so many pagan rites, this fixed sign, this educator, comes to be known as The Pope.

What is the role of myth relative to education? Is it the duty of education to recognize it, or perpetuate it?

This is my Hierophant: With a red robe of knowledge, acceptance, and intuition. The numeral five denotes the senses, physical vehicles of passion. On the forehead the numeral three: Justice, Strength, and Temperance. Instruments of science survive the ancient popes who sought to stifle them. A student breathes these in, curious, or exhales them, having learned.

Dogma best serves man when it serves the values of peace.

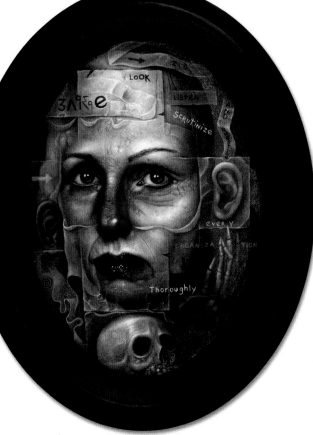

"The Anti-Lemming"

"Bent Cross Svengali"

"Auto-Intervention"

"Corporatocracy Queen"

"End Times of the Armageddonist"

"In Preparation for Barrier Transcendence"

"Resurrection Machine"

"Something Empty"

"Flushing the Celebration of Ignorance"

"To Vanquish Dogma"

"The Medicine Show"

"P.O.G."

"The Attic"

CHRISTOPHER UMANA

www.christopherumana.com

"A Melancholic Discovery"

·VI·
THE LOVERS

I incorporated myself into the piece by using the Costa Rican Resplendent Quetzal to represent my ethnic background. The Costa Rican Heliconious Melpomene, or "postman butterfly," to represent the angel watching over The Lovers and blessing the bond between the couple with his powerful rays of light which symbolize the highest state of consciousness. I used the butterfly because while doing research, I found that it is a multi-cultural symbol of a carrier of souls to the afterlife. The birds show their connection, bond, or union by opening themselves and sharing their essences with each other. This also fits the triangular shape of the original card which symbolized the dilemma of being tempted between right and wrong. The berries and flames symbolize the intoxication of the material world, and their clothing is meant to mimic the birds' plumage in the natural world.

"Tomboy Tom-Foolery"

"Punto De Coyuntura"

"Rebirth of Venus"

"The Siren's Cetacean Aria"

"A Wedge of Cranes"

"In the Void"

"The Moonwort Elucidation"

" Legend of the Begetter"

"The Reaper"

"Come to Daddy"

"Sanctified Fortitude"

"The Ankle-Biter Epiphany"

"The World"

"Második Galamb"

"The Chariot"

CHRISTOPHER CONN ASKEW

www.sekretcity.com

"Annunciation"

·VII·
THE CHARIOT

The Chariot card has always had a special attraction to me visually, so I was very pleased to be assigned that card. After some consideration, I decided not to alter the subject imagery too much, because I like the way the traditional forms, which have been handed down for centuries, have so many interpretations depending on the user; the way that, over the years, interpretations change, but the basic imagery remains constant. In all of my work, I strive to express a continuity of culture over time, a sense of tradition that is remolded by new ideas, so I tried to approach the subject from that angle, as opposed to taking a very personal (and therefore modern) reading of the card's meaning.

"Eqvvs Novissimvs"

"M96"

ET ENSUITE, LORSQUE LE SOIR AVANÇAIT...

"Fox"

"Queen of Diamonds"

"Six Girls"

"Kshatriya"

"La Croix Rouge"

"Carmelia"

"ALVB"

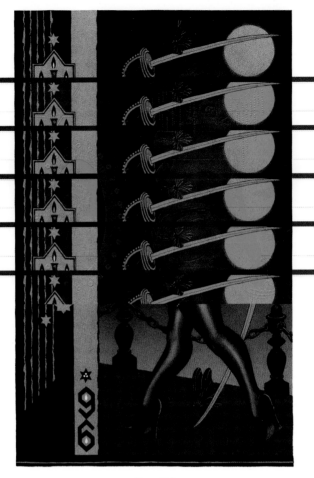

"Arcadia"

"Maschere"

"B.Z.G."

"Strength"

BRIAN M. VIVEROS

www.brianmviveros.com

·VII·
STRENGTH

She is strength, she is determined, she is power, she is the focused smoking soldier that has walked through the battlefields of life.

She is confident within herself and presents herself to the world as strong. Her cuts and scars are a reminder of what she's been through, and through it all, she is a survivor standing tall.

"The Last Temptation"

"Bull-Fight-Her"

"Momma Said Knock You Out"

"Unclean"

"Bleed For Me"

"Scorpio Rizing"

"Hang Over"

"La Carnivora"

"Viva La Muerte I"

"Mess with the Bull"

"Bloody Knuckles"

"Mata – Adore You Forever"

"Captain Howdy"

"Night-Stalk-Her"

CLAUDIA DRAKE

www.urgentalchemy.com

·IX·
THE HERMIT

I work by chance and the compass of my own intuition. This project was an unexpected challenge for me. In the push to follow set translations of my card, I found an unconscious pull to veer off topic. The more the push the larger the pull. My final piece is a fusion of established translations of the card, built from the angle of context to symbol, inside-out.

"Fire Walk With Me"

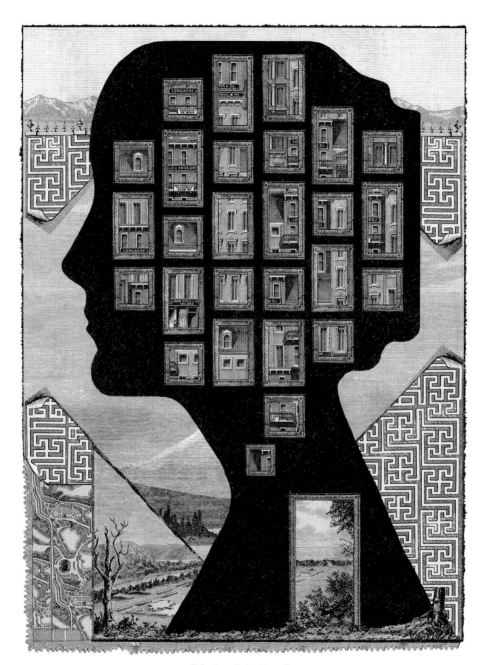

"The Search for Home"

"Voyeur"

"Moira"

"Inside the Dreaming"

"Lady in Waiting"

"Wheel of Fortune"

www.heatherwatts.com

"Sun Goddess"

"The Weary Shepherd"

·X·
WHEEL OF FORTUNE

This painting began in my mind as a hazy vision of characters moving in a complex and colorful arrangement around a central wheel. When I first sat down to determine a color scheme and sketch out the basics, I found myself at a loss. I knew the essence of the painting, but the individuals and symbols comprising it were largely still a mystery to me. As I fumbled along trying to bridge the gap between the elaborate but vague image in my head and the blank canvas in front of me, the meaning of the card struck home. The Wheel of Fortune is about change and movement, destiny and opportunity, expectation, perspective and direction. It isn't about best laid plans and linear progressions. I was going to have to pack up the tidy, step-by-step creative process I'd envisioned for this huge undertaking and fling it out to the mercy of fortune. In doing so I would make the card's theme central not only to the image I was painting, but to the process of painting itself.

Trusting in the dictates of the card to guide my work, I relinquished control. I let go of trying to plan things and became flexible, taking advantage of chance, luck, and opportunity—all facets of the card's meaning. By reminding myself that things can change and connect in unexpected ways—another central aspect of the card—I was able to see how seemingly dissonant half-finished images had the potential to draw together into a cohesive, meaningful and faithful representation of the card.

Anchoring myself in this process, I watched as, over a period of approximately six weeks, the characters around the wheel slowly emerged— first like ghosts, sketched roughly in paint, and eventually in crisp detail, demanding a diverse palette of colors. Sometimes these characters arose only to depart, somehow not fitting with the larger intent of the work. Other times space had to be made to insert imagery that seemed integral to the piece, even though I had only just thought of it. I was amazed by the way that each new addition to the painting seemed to spark other ideas, and also by the slow, plodding, puzzle-piece way that things gradually snapped together to form the finished work.

In the final result, the characters directly around the wheel experience different fortunes from different perspectives, but all are caught up in an interconnected, moving, changing cycle. The figures in the corners symbolize forces divine or natural outside of our control, and are specifically tied to the elements of earth, wind, water and fire. The Wheel of Fortune is historically said to be turned by the Goddess Fortuna, and in her spirit these corner figures provide a feminine counterpoint to the more masculine characters on the wheel.

"The Rat King"

"Green Eggs & Ham"

"New Gods"

"She Sees Things Differently"

"Beneath the Surface"

"Bumper Cars"

"Insert Coin"

"Pearls of Wisdom"

"Self Portrait"

"The Pale Horse Finds His Calling"

"The Red Menace"

"The Squirrel"

"Justice"

MOLLY CRABAPPLE

www.mollycrabapple.com

"Art Monkeys"

·XI·
JUSTICE

For the Justice card, my piggies climb a blind justice's spiral staircase, and sometimes jump off…

"Octopus Girl"

"Octopus Girl Two"

"Dorian Deconstructed #1"

"Dorian Deconstructed #2"

"Hanged Man"

"Octopus"

"The Box"

"Coilhouse"

"Portrait of Amber Ray"

"Storyville"

"The Hanged Man"

·XII·
THE HANGED MAN

I began the painting by doing a photo shoot with Aprella; from there I moved over to sketching it out on the panel before painting with oils.

LAURIE LIPTON

laurielipton.com

·XIII·
DEATH

The horror of my idea for the Death Card was the skeletal horse. Drawing a man's bones is hard enough, but a horse's? Then there was the landscape filled with bodies... well, that was easy/peasy compared to the horse. In the traditional interpretation of the card, Death doesn't only mean The End... It can also mean getting rid of the old in order to make way for a new beginning. That is why I put the flowers reaching up and out between the barren bones in the earth. There is a rising sun in the background. The headstones are turning into a city as they move towards the horizon and the dawn: death and night turning into the hustle and bustle of life and light. The scythe is glowing like the sun and is animated by its rays: life to death again. Round and round and round we go...

"Collateral Damage"

"Time Travel"

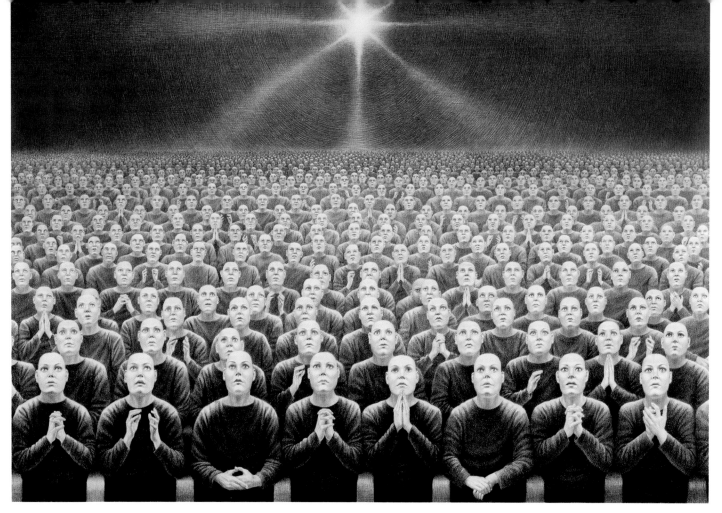

"Delusion Dwellers"

"Death & the Maiden"

"Facelift"

"Info Glut"

"Lachrymose Lace"

"Family Reunion"

"Love Bite"

"Mirror, Mirror"

"Off Spring"

"Senorita Muerte"

"On"

"Prime Time"

"Surveillance"

"Temperance"

PATRICK "STAR 27" DEIGNAN

www.artstar27.com

"Bad Obsession"

·XIV·
TEMPERANCE

For most of my life I have been a person of extremes. My personal art deals with the most dramatic of human emotions, vices, and taboos. It is not only a job, but an obsession that I pour all of myself into. My past has left me with a health problem. While most of my vices have been arrested, I tend to still treat myself with reckless abandon. Ironically, this card was chosen for me at a time when I had gone beyond my bounds, pushing myself to pull together a new body of work. My body, my relationships, and my entire well-being had suffered. I began research on the Tarot and trying to pull together some ideas.

It was difficult at first to figure out how to make a card that represents balance and needs to portray a sense of serenity fit my style. However, things began to fall in place. Once the sketch was on the canvas, I was extremely pleased.

Unfortunately, no major life-changing peacefulness descended on my life in the act of creating. Towards the end, I had begun forcing healthier work days. During the process, I learned that my father was dying from cancer. This brought a lot of distress and fitful periods of work followed by long periods of grief.

Upon completion of the card, I actually began to make my life much more balanced. Of course, life shows up, and things change.

"The Day the Toymaker's Only Tool Was a Hammer"

"Pieta"

"Bitter"

"Somber Mourning"

"Comforting Misery"

"Offering"

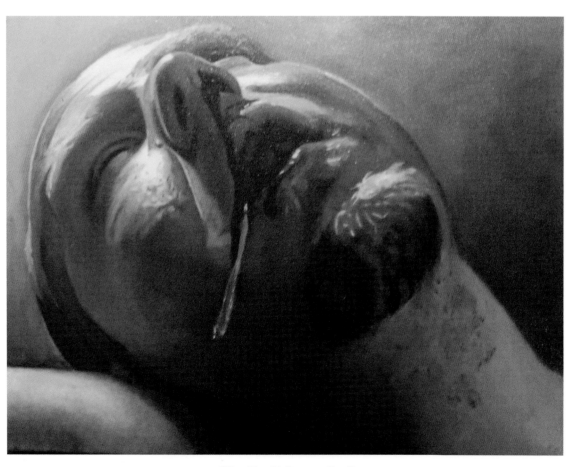

"Now I Lay Me Down to Sleep"

"Courage"

"Defiled Conception"

"V"

"Judge Me Not"

"Misery Loves Company"

"The Devil"

CHET ZAR

·XV·
THE DEVIL

My card is a kind of postmodern take on The Devil from the Rider-Smith-Waite deck (which is derived from Eliphas Levi's illustration "Baphomet") using my own personal iconography – gas masks, guns, and flat heads.

"Death Plays Air Guitar On A Scythe"

"Black Magick"

"Choke"

"Fiend"

"I Want You"

"Runt"

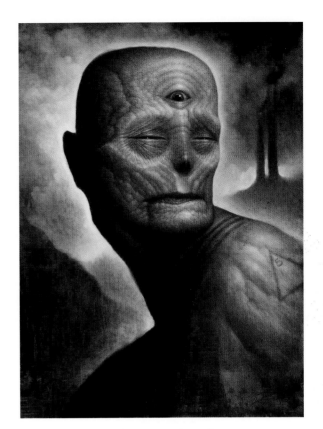

"Shamanic Tendencies"

"Succubus"

"Lilith"

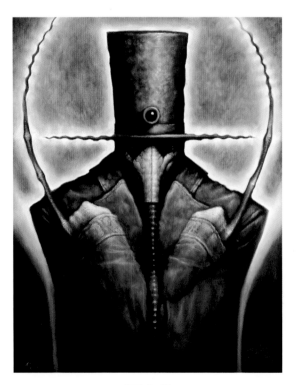

"Warlock"

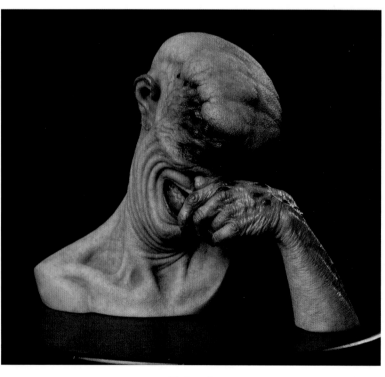

"Softspot"

"Crybaby"

"Lilith and Her Owl Familiar"

"Crow Girl"

"Dragonlady"

"The Tower"

JESSICA JOSLIN

www.jessicajoslin.com

·XVI·
THE TOWER

The Tower card is an omen that falsely held beliefs are about to come crashing down. In this interpretation, I looked to imagery that haunted me as a child: A Night on Bald Mountain, from Walt Disney's Fantasia. In it, a bucolic mountainside transforms, with the setting of the sun, into a bat-like demon. I imagined the Tower itself unfurling and turning into a bat creature. As its wings open, the chains attached to the wings and to the tower begin to tear the fortress apart. The bat is representative of the hubris inherent in false belief, that which eventually necessitates it's destruction.

"Lucky"

"Rudolph"

"Cooper"

Druscilla

"Quentin"

"Clio and Loci"

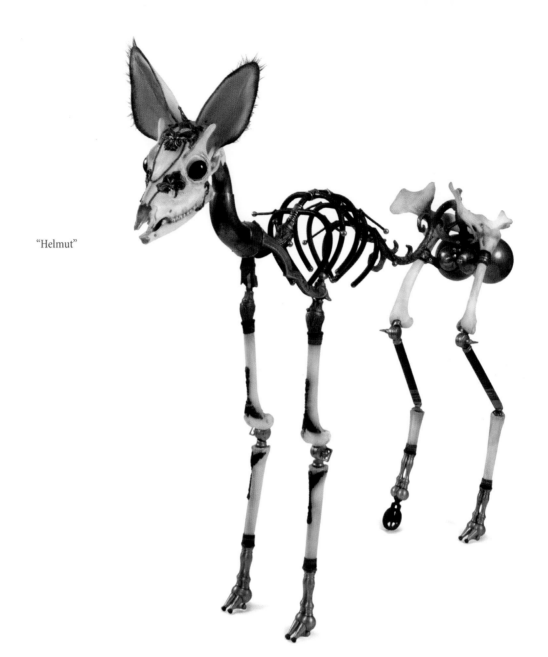

"Helmut"

"Lautrec"

"Violet and Cordula"

JESSICA JOSLIN

"Gustav"

"The Star"

DANNI SHINYA LUO

www.dshinya.blogspot.com

"Youth and Her Glory"

·XVII·
THE STAR

I was very excited to find out that I was assigned the Star card in the Lowbrow Tarot Cards project. I've worked with Tarot Cards before. So, this time, I really wanted to incorporate more symbolism into the painting. First step was to do some research on the card, find out what THE STAR means. After that, I took all the meanings and simplified them down to single words. Then I looked up all the cultural/mythical icons that represented those key words, and began to compose them visually. It was kind of a perfect fit that The Star was traditionally represented by a woman, because female figures are the main subject matters of my paintings. I composed the symbols around the woman in the center focus, such as the robin eggs and seashells in her hair, the flock of doves flying in the back; and then everything against the lotus pond in the background. All together, these objects make up the complete meaning of the Star card, while at the same time, are aesthetically pleasing.

"Two of a Kind"

"Love's Secret"

"Chaotic Harmony"

"Beast"

"Crowded by Emptiness"

"A Thousand Hands to Touch Your Soul"

"Cosmic Circus"

"One Lick to Paradise"

"Desire"

"Play Nice"

"Duality"

"The Moon"

JENNYBIRD ALCANTARA

www.jennybirdart.com

·XVIII·
THE MOON

The Moon card came to me in a serendipitous way. After being offered that particular card to interpret, I reviewed some sketches that I had been working on some months earlier and came upon drawings of a woman's head surrounded by wolves. These ideas hadn't yet worked themselves into a painting and it seemed coincidental that without knowing what card I would get, the one offered me had already been scheming itself onto the pages of my sketchbook. Not to mention the crayfish that stood ferociously in my path, one day during this same time period while I was walking at the park, causing me to jump back in fright, thinking it was a scorpion! Not only were the images I had been working on in line with the Moon card, but upon doing further research about the meaning of the card itself, it became very clear to me why I "pulled" this one.

The Moon card deals with anxiety and fear and the release of inner demons as well as mystery and illusion. I feel a deep connection to the aspects of this card so it was fortuitous that I should be chosen for this one in particular. My interpretation focuses on the mystery and journey into the unknown. My work in general has, at its core, a dreamlike narrative, and through my paintings, I contemplate the complex interconnectedness of opposites as seen through the prism of myth, fable, and fantasy. The anthropomorphic qualities of my characters show the relationship of the central figure to the world she inhabits.

So, in my depiction of the Moon card, the wolves aren't separate from the Moon; they are connected to her through the tangle of vines sprouting from her mind and plunging into the waters of the subconscious below. The moon has a dark aspect depicted by the snarling animal in her keyhole belly but at the same time she is holding a sleeping bunny doll which, for me, is a symbol of safety and protection. The journey into the night is fraught with danger but beyond the dark path and out of the deep pools there is a golden horizon, lending assurance to the wanderer that the journey is worth the risks involved.

"Treacherous Gardens"

JENNYBIRD ALCANTARA

"Swooning at the River of Oblivion"

"More Mischief in the Thicket"

"The Duel"

"Bo-Peep"

"Reviving Ophelia"

"Sleepwalker"

"Mary's Little Lamb"

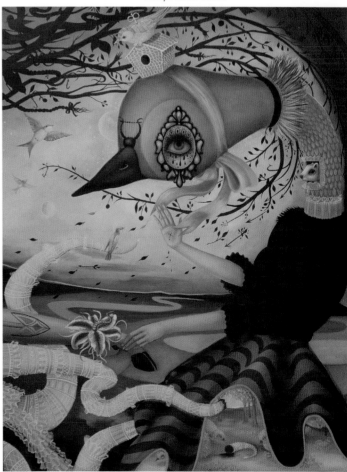

"Struggle in the Garden of the Porcelain Queen"

"Truce"

"The Journey"

"Making Fast Friends in Dreamland"

"Talisman"

"The Sun"

ANGIE MASON

www.angiemason.com

"Proletariat's Breakdown"

·XIX·
THE SUN

The Tarot, like life, is so full of chance and it is very fitting how I came to find myself with The Sun card – or more like The Sun card found me through a series of events. But it has turned out to be the card I needed to take on. I feel very fortunate being a part of this project; since I was young, the Tarot always held a place of mystery and fascination. I believe the Tarot can simply aid one in sorting out life issues suggesting themes we all struggle with by highlighting them through a reading. The Tarot is not mere magic to me, it's more of a way to meditate and focus in on certain aspects of your life, unlocking something within yourself, bringing greater attention toward solving and moving past issues. Having The Sun card find me was a form of enlightenment, opening me up to realizations about life and people through acceptance of situations. It helped me meditate on expanding outward a brilliance of self-assured happiness discovering one's own voice. I found a personal power within myself during a transitory time breaking free from certain personal walls that were holding me back, which caused me to find that greater self-assurance and optimism about my future. My personal journey was extremely cathartic using this card to really symbolize all that I was dealing with. This card was really about focusing in on positivity and exploding negativity outward away from one's center and letting positive rays of light shine down, opening one up for new growth. By remaining open, one moves past negative situations, allowing oneself to embrace the joyful energy and opportunities life has to offer.

"Sour Loser in a Bit of a Pickle"

"Industry Vomits"

ANGIE MASON

"Consumption Malfunction"

"Not So Magical More Like a Mess"

"Pendulum Plague"

"Sweet Defeat"

"Some Magic Left in Me"

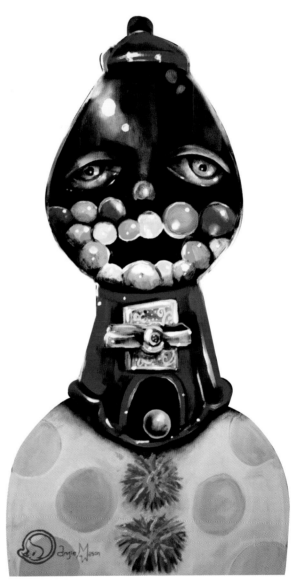

"When Giving Leaves You Empty"

"The Royal Pain of Potential Colony Collapse"

"Deceit Tree"

"Dealt Hand"

"Swing the Heartache"

"Rot Stopper – Too Rotted To Live Too Ripe To Die"

"Momentary Lapse Of Living"

"Judgment"

SCOTT G. BROOKS

www.scottgbrooks.com

"Maternal Instincts"

JUDGMENT

The Judgment card is about change, resurrection, and facing our past.

The Angel tells the fool, "Each step wears down the shoe just a bit, and so shapes the next step you take, and the next and the next. Your past is always under your feet. You cannot hide from it, run from it, or rid yourself of it. But you can call it up, and come to terms with it."

I was about to move to a new apartment, and the act of going through each and every possession had forced me to confront my past. I literally could not move forward until I reviewed all the remnants of past relationships, work projects, and family issues. Items need to be either thrown away, given away, sold, or packed up. Each item has its own history and an uncanny ability to reconnect me with past events. Space is limited, so each decision requires deliberation. It would be so much easier to box everything up without a thought and store it away in some shadowy corner.

I had been in my current home studio for just about ten years. It's been an amazing decade of change and growth not only in my career, but also in my family and relationships. Even in the midst of that change, there have been times when I saw myself living here forever. There are others in this building who have been here for over fifty years. Letting go of a sense of place, let alone just the material stuff, has always been difficult for me. This has been a challenging experience, but the process is clearing the way for a fresh start.

SCOTT G. BROOKS

"We the People"

"Battle for Thorazine"

"Food Chain"

"Family Way"

"Patience"

"Duty Bound in a Fancy Coat"

"Boldly Going"

"Breaking Up Is Hard To Do"

"Royally Ducked"

"Family Affair"

"The World"

AUNIA KAHN

www.auniakahn.com

"Burnt Fuel"

·XXI·
THE WORLD

After the completion of the Silver Era Tarot deck with author Russell J. Moon, who wrote the accompanied companion book, I wanted to explore Tarot further. I was approached by many artists over the four and a half years during and after completion, ecstatic at my ability to create 78 original works of art, sticking to the traditional symbolism of Tarot and publishing a deck, who expressed interest in doing the same; but lacked the time, and other commitments kept them from satisfying this curiosity. I agree it was a fulfilling accomplishment, but a very large undertaking and I felt I wanted to share with others artists, and create another journey for them to be a part of. This thought birthed the idea to bring together some of my favorite and extremely talented creative people to create a deck with each artist exploring one card, and using their unique artist ability to create their interpretation of their card of choice.

With the idea in place, it was time for me to choose a card that best fit me. I was drawn to The Star, which has always been a card I adored for very personal reasons. I was happy with my decision until I started to work with it in the form of creativity and the pull was just not there. Stumbling over my own choice, I looked further to find the card that really suited me and the project, The World [XXI]. The World is the final card of the Major Arcana sequential journey, representing an ending to a cycle of life, a pause in life before the next cycle begins with The Fool. This seemed so fitting since I just completed my own deck, and now onto this new and amazing project with others to form a new journey.

AUNIA KAHN

"Exit Ghost"

"American Political"

"Flight of the Ceraunograph"

"Salutary Absorption"

"Descent Into Madness"

"Story of Ruins"

"Nurturing Ingenuity"

"Viral Tropism"

"Royal Academy"

"Caelum Heights"

Conclusion

Many thanks to all who supported, worked, and strived to bring this magnificent project to life.